S0-CFD-637

THE NUCLEAR DISASTER AT CHERNOBYL

ROBIN CRUISE

Artesian **Press**

P.O. Box 355 Buena Park, CA 90621

Take Ten Books
Disaster

Other Take Ten Themes:

Mystery

Sports

Adventure

Chillers

Thrillers

Romance

Horror

Fantasy

Project Editor: Dwayne Epstein
Assistant Editor: Molly Mraz
Graphic Design: Tony Amaro
Cover photo courtesy of ITAR/TASS
©2003 Artesian Press

www.artesianpress.com

 **Artesian Press**   ISBN 1-58659-022-7

CONTENTS

Chapter 1

Technicians at a nuclear power plant near Stockholm, Sweden, were puzzled. They discovered higher than normal levels of radiation in the atmosphere on Sunday, April 27, 1986.

The technicians searched for an answer to this dangerous mystery. They traced the wind and weather patterns that had brought spring rains and snow to the area. They saw that the weather, and the nuclear fallout that blew in with it, had come from their neighbor to the south: the Soviet Union.

An accident had occurred in the Soviet Union that was sending dangerous levels of nuclear radiation to areas as far away as Sweden. What was happening in the Soviet Union?

Four days later, red flags lined the streets of Moscow in celebration of May Day. It was cool and windy that Thursday. Mikhail S. Gorbachev, leader of the Soviet Union at the time, wore a hat and light coat to protect himself from the wind.

Still, the breeze carried with it the promise of spring, and thousands of marchers filed through Red Square. It was the start of the four-day-long May Day celebration, a dual holiday in the U.S.S.R. In addition to marking the arrival of spring, the annual pageant also honors the workers of the world.

Gorbachev smiled and waved to greet the people of Moscow and other patriotic citizens who had turned out for the celebration. It appeared that he had reason to be happy. After all, his rule had marked the start of a new era in the Soviet Union—an era known for *glasnost*, or openness.

On that spring day nearly anything seemed possible. With Gorbachev leading the U.S.S.R., world leaders at last had reason to hope that a new spirit of cooperation would replace the secrecy and suspicion of almost three decades.

The world welcomed the possibility of peace. Even the United States, under the leadership of President Ronald Reagan, seemed to believe that the two supernations could put aside some of their differences. Then they could help the other nations of the world move forward together.

Gorbachev had taken over as leader in 1985. He was younger than many of the officials who had gone before him at the Kremlin (Russian government). He had a reputation for being very different from the leaders who had guided the Soviet Union in the past. Millions of citizens scattered throughout the Soviet republics believed he had a better sense of the problems and needs of the many peoples in this enormous country.

As is often the case, however, things were not exactly as they seemed on that spring day in 1986. Even as Gorbachev smiled and waved amid the pageantry of May Day, a gloomy drama was unfolding in Ukraine and Belarus, two Slavic republics in the western U.S.S.R.

Although he had a new policy of glasnost, Gorbachev had said very little about the situation. The May Day celebration was not a good time to talk about a serious accident. Even on that spring day, with Gorbachev greeting the crowds, many Russians did not know that a deadly chain of events had been set in motion the previous Saturday. The explosion that had occurred at the Chernobyl Nuclear Power Plant would shake the Soviet Union—and the rest of the world—for many years.

Chapter 2

The Chernobyl Nuclear Power Plant opened in 1983 in a republic called Ukraine. The massive power plant seemed out of place in the wooded countryside and farmlands surrounding it, but the need for the plant was clear: It provided a much-needed boost in electrical energy for the people who lived in Belarus and Ukraine.

The nuclear power plant served the community of Chernobyl and the forty-five thousand people who lived nearby in Pripyat. The plant also generated electricity for the 2.5 million residents of the Ukrainian capital of Kiev, eighty miles to the south.

On April 26, 1986, four reactors were

operating at Chernobyl. Two more reactors were under construction. The Soviets had big plans for the Chernobyl plant: When all six reactors were in full operation, it would be one of the most powerful energy sources in the Soviet Union.

Like any nuclear power source of that size, the Chernobyl plant had the potential for disaster as well as power. A nuclear accident could cause deadly radiation to contaminate the region and areas beyond.

Like many other nuclear reactors through the Soviet Union, the four RBMK-1000 units at Chernobyl were powerful machines. They depended on technology that had been standard throughout much of the Soviet Union for more than thirty years. (The "1000" means that when operating at full capacity, the reactor yields 1000 megawatts of electricity—enough to light a city the size of Toledo, Ohio.)

Although many Soviet engineers believed the design of the Chernobyl plant was good, other nuclear specialists thought that the RBMK-1000 was outdated and possibly dangerous. Some believed that the design of the RBMK-1000 might result in serious health risks—even the loss of lives—if an accident occurred.

In the RBMK-1000, the reactor is kept going by fission, but the uranium rods are regulated with graphite instead of water. Graphite can be dangerous. If it catches fire, it burns with a white-hot heat that can fuel an uncontrollable meltdown of the reactor core. A meltdown happens when the fuel rods begin to melt. (Except for one unit in Washington state, reactors throughout the U.S. rely on pressurized water rather than graphite to control the rate of activity in the core. Water has the ability to cool the reactor more quickly.) In addition, some evidence shows that the RBMK-1000 is unstable when it operates at low power. Workers at Chernobyl had planned to shift into low power for a test at the plant in April 1986.

Others were concerned that the design for the Chernobyl plant did not include a containment structure. It works as a safety net that might prevent radioactive materials from being released directly into the atmosphere during an accident.

The containment structure at Three Mile Island in Pennsylvania had kept down the release of radioactive materials following the partial meltdown there in 1979. That accident taught scientists that a containment structure could mean the difference between life and death for thousands of people caught in the nightmare of a nuclear accident.

Chapter 3

The night of Friday, April 25, 1986, was clear and star-filled in Ukraine. If it seemed to be business as usual at Chernobyl, that was not the case. Still, it was not until hours before dawn on Saturday, April 26—1:23 a.m., to be exact—that Chernobyl plunged into the depths of the worst disaster in the history of nuclear energy.

The Soviets had been planning to conduct a generator test at the Chernobyl plant. This meant that the RBMK-1000 would operate at reduced power. To conduct the test, workers at Chernobyl turned off many emergency systems. They removed the rods used to control the rate of nuclear activity in the graphite core. As it turned out, there was an increase rather than a reduction of power in the core. That burst of energy caused an unstoppable chain reaction.

When the water that cooled the uranium fuel rods dipped to levels too low to work well, the fuel rods overheated in a partial "meltdown" of the core. The extreme heat of the steam then caused an explosion that blasted open the roof of Unit 4. Oxygen from the outside air fueled a fire in the graphite core. The fire released a deadly cloud of radioactive particles into the atmosphere.

Lieutenant Colonel Leonid Telyatnikov was called to Chernobyl at 1:32 a.m. He was in charge of the twenty-eight firefighters who tried hard to put out the raging fire in the Unit 4 reactor.

With the reactor caught in a blaze of extreme heat, it is easy to see why

Lieutenant Colonel Telyatnikov and his crew could not put out that fire at Chernobyl. As it turned out, it took more than a week for the fire in the reactor to burn out. During that week, millions of people around the world could only watch, struggling to understand how bad the disaster really was.

Chapter 4

The scene that Telyatnikov and his brave team faced must have seemed like a nightmare. Some thirty fires were burning at the site, with bursts of flames flashing into the darkness like sparklers. Unit 4 was burning out of control. The air had the heavy smell of burnt metal. Blue flames shot more than two thousand feet skyward and a dangerous smoke billowed three miles up into the atmosphere. It carried with it deadly forms of radioactive particles.

The explosive heat had blasted through the thousand-pound lid of the reactor. The blast had torn through the

An aerial view of the Chernobyl Nuclear Power Plant taken May ninth. The arrow shows the charred remains of the Unit 4 reactor, where the accident occurred.

17

roof of the 230-foot-tall building that housed Unit 4. The temperature in the core of the reactor, where the graphite was burning white-hot, was hotter than five thousand degrees (twice the temperature needed to melt steel).

Lieutenant Colonel Telyatnikov and his crew had only water hoses to fight the blaze. They wore no special gear to protect themselves from the radiation released in the fire. There was not time to discuss the serious danger––the invisible threat of radiation––so the firefighters immediately went to work.

Although there was no way they could put out the flames, they managed to keep the fires from spreading beyond the plant. By 5:00 a.m., all of the fires, except for the one in the reactor, had been put out. By dawn, as Telyatnikov and some of the other firefighters began to vomit, the horror of their nightmare began to take shape: radiation poisoning.

Many of the firefighters suffered burns on their hands, faces, and other exposed areas of their bodies. Some would have severe liver problems, and six of them would be dead within ten weeks. Two workers died at the site— one from burns, the other after being struck by falling materials. The deaths related directly to the Chernobyl disaster eventually would climb to thirty-two. Hundreds of people were hospitalized, and hundreds of cases of radiation poisoning resulted from the accident.

Those deaths and reported illnesses were part of a chapter in nuclear history that could have serious results for generations to come. It was a disaster that dumped fifty tons of radioactive particles and burning graphite into the atmosphere.

Thousands of people in Belarus, which absorbed seventy percent of the contamination that fell in the Soviet

Union, were exposed to high levels of radiation.

Only time will tell how they will be affected by the radiation.

Chapter 5

Soviet officials did not immediately comment on the terrible events that had taken place at Chernobyl. But by Monday morning, April 28, the world had learned that a nuclear disaster had occurred.

The Soviets at first denied that there was a problem. They later said that there had been an accident, but did not provide any more information.

Gorbachev did not comment on the situation for almost three days. Finally, at 9:00 p.m. on Monday, April 28—nearly three days after the explosion in Unit 4—a Soviet newscaster read a brief statement from the Council of Ministers. The statement said that an accident had taken place at the Chernobyl power station, and one of the reactors was damaged. They were trying to clean up the accident area and were offering help to those who needed it. A government team had been set up to investigate.

Tass, the official Soviet newspaper, offered little information: "An explosion destroyed the building housing the reactor, and a fire broke out. That happened at night. After the explosion, the engine room took fire . . . Radioactivity was released upwards, and then a fire started inside."

During the next ten days, fallout blew north toward Scandinavia. Radioactive material then was carried south and east. The winds and winter weather reduced the nuclear fallout throughout Europe. Still, world leaders were angry that Soviet officials had not immediately shared the news of the disaster.

At first, the official response from the Soviets was that they did not want to alarm others needlessly until they knew all the facts. They said their first job had been to figure out what had happened and if people were at risk because of the accident.

Soviet officials also said that the situation at Chernobyl was under control, though Unit 4 continued to burn for days. It was not until the week's end—after military helicopters had dumped five thousand tons of boron, clay, and sand to smother the heat—that the fire burned itself out.

Glasnost, it appeared, had been ignored. Gorbachev was under attack. As the Soviets declined offers of help from other nations, including the U.S., worry quickly turned to anger. There was talk that the Soviets were trying to cover up the serious results of the disaster.

Speaking in a radio address from Tokyo, President Ronald Reagan said at the end of the first week after the accident, "The Soviets owe the world an explanation. A full account of what happened at Chernobyl and what is happening now is the least the world community has a right to expect."

Because so few details were available soon after the meltdown, nations that believed they might be affected by nuclear fallout began to panic for a little while. Some took extreme measures to protect themselves.

Romania declared a "state of alert" and warned people not to drink rainwater. Polish officials stopped the sale of milk from cows fed on grass that may have been affected by nuclear fallout. Residents of Scandinavia worried about feeding their children fresh fruits and vegetables.

As time passed, however, it became clear that even throughout Europe, exposure to radiation carried by the wind from Chernobyl had been relatively mild.

Europeans may have received one to ten *millirem* of radiation. (The radiation from a typical chest X-ray is twenty millirem.) People in the western U.S.S.R. and parts of Scandinavia may have been exposed to radiation in excess of ten millirem. A tiny increase in radioactivity was detected in California, though there was almost no direct impact on the United States.

As it turned out, fallout from Chernobyl did not harm most of the world. The radiation did harm thousands of people who worked at the plant or lived in areas of Ukraine and Belarus affected by nuclear fallout.

Early estimates of deaths in those regions were unreliable. Later estimates were more accurate. However, it may be impossible to determine how many people died as a result of the events that took place at Chernobyl on April 26, 1986.

Chapter 6

Even residents of Ukraine and nearby Belarus had little sense of the invisible—and perhaps deadly—threat they faced. Some residents of Ukraine first learned of the accident from radio programs from nearby Poland.

Five years after the accident, a nine-year-old radiation victim recalled, "We first didn't know there was an accident. Then we thought some kind of machine had exploded. Or just everything exploded. We didn't know."

Health risks caused by exposure to high levels of radiation are serious. The closer and longer the exposure, the greater the risks. People who lived in Pripyat—which once had forty-five thousand residents, including many of the 7,500 workers who worked at the Chernobyl plant—were very close indeed. Most of them were not moved from the area until thirty-six hours after the disaster, long after being exposed to high levels of radiation.

After being alerted, the residents of Pripyat had no choice but to move quickly. They packed what they could carry and got on the 1,100 buses the government provided. They had to leave their homes and the lives they had known.

Many had to leave their belongings behind. Laundry was left flapping in the wind as they made their quick exit. Beloved family pets were left behind. Contaminated farm animals were slaughtered.

Eventually, the Soviet government would relocate 166,000 citizens who lived in contaminated areas within a nineteen-mile radius of the Chernobyl

Nearly two months after the accident, a helicopter sprays a decontaminating substance over the region surrounding the Chernobyl Nuclear Power Plant.

plant. New communities, such as Slavutich (built to house 30,000 people), sprang up almost overnight. Soviet laborers discovered it was possible to build a house in forty-five days.

Six hundred thousand workers were called in to begin the massive cleanup at the energy station and the area surrounding it. They wore special coveralls and masks to protect themselves. Gorbachev told them their task was "to liquidate the consequences of the accident." They became known as the *likividatory*.

Because nuclear decay will continue for hundreds of years in the core, the blown reactor was covered with steel and concrete. People worked in round-the-clock shifts for more than six months to seal in possible contamination.

The huge power plant was cleared of rubble. It was scrubbed down and freshly painted. The land surrounding it was scrubbed and cleaned. (Contaminated topsoil was sealed in enormous drums and hauled away.) In January 1987, Chernobyl was deemed a safe place to work. This was done by Dr. Morris Rosen, an American who was the safety director of the International Atomic Energy Agency.

The difficult job of the likividatory also included keeping contamination from going into the Pripyat River. The river is the main water source for millions of citizens. Miners tunneled beneath the reactor, which sat near the river.

They reinforced the structure with concrete so that it would not sink into the earth beneath the weight of the lead, sand, and clay dumped on the fire. If the reactor had sunk into the land near the river, the water would have become contaminated, transporting the nuclear waste to areas across the country.

No official price tag has been attached to the massive cleanup effort, which continued full-force for the better part of a year. Western officials have estimated the cost to be billions of dollars.

Familiar daily life for thousands of citizens ended in the weeks and months after the accident. Schools closed early for the year. Thousands of children were shipped off to camps and resorts in clean areas far away from Chernobyl. Parents in Kiev were advised to limit their children's outdoor play to an hour a day. Residents of some areas were told to bathe often. Some placed damp rags at the doorways to their homes so that they could clean the radioactive dust from their shoes before entering.

Portions of the richest farmland in the Soviet Union had been contaminated. Fruits and vegetables were regularly checked for radiation. Residents of contaminated areas were given safe food and water. Selling produce from contaminated land was a crime in some areas.

More than thirteen thousand acres of agricultural land had been contaminated. Radioactive particles released at Chernobyl decay very slowly. That means the exposed farmland will remain contaminated for many years. Huge water trucks drove down the streets of Kiev and other communities. They sprayed water from their hoses night and day in an effort to flush away nuclear fallout.

The water in many areas was unsafe to drink. Some food was unsafe to eat. Millions of dollars' worth of fruits and vegetables that may have been contaminated were thrown away.

Chapter 7

Dr. Robert Gale was a pioneer in a very specialized form of surgery. He was an expert at transplanting bone marrow. Bone marrow produces the blood that circulates through and nourishes the human body. For someone who has been exposed to a deadly dose of radiation, injecting healthy marrow into the body can mean the difference between life and death.

Dr. Gale was responsible for running many bone marrow transplant centers throughout the world. Five days after he learned of the Chernobyl disaster, he boarded a plane for Moscow. It would be weeks before he returned to his wife and three young children in California.

The forty-year-old Los Angeles surgeon knew he could help Soviet doctors treat victims who suffered from extreme radiation poisoning. Dr. Gale also understood there was no time to waste. The doctors knew that they had to operate as soon as possible—within a week or two—in order to save lives. The longer the delay in replacing bone marrow, the more likely death became.

Dr. Gale and his Russian colleagues immediately began to check the three hundred radiation victims who had been sent to a hospital in Moscow. These were the firemen, guards, and workers who had been exposed directly to the blast. The doctors had $800,000 worth of special equipment shipped in so that they could do the difficult surgery.

Dr. Gale also arranged to have his favorite bagels shipped to Moscow from Los Angeles. Maybe the bagels gave him extra strength during the long hours he worked so far from home. He was checked by a Geiger counter, a special machine that tests radiation levels. It was done each time he left the ward to make sure he was not spreading the contamination.

The patients Dr. Gale treated were very ill. Many of them had lost their hair and were sick to their stomachs. Others had bad diarrhea or high fevers. The sickest patients had many of those symptoms. Dr. Gale and the Russian doctors did thirteen bone marrow transplants. Five of their patients were saved from death.

Dr. Gale understood that his mission had two purposes: to help the sick and to demonstrate the West's concern about the events at Chernobyl. Through all the long, dark hours he worked side by side with the Russian surgeons, his motto had been "nothing is impossible." The Russian newspaper Pravda praised the surgeon's work.

Chapter 8

The most serious health risks from nuclear fallout occur within the first few weeks of a disaster, such as the one at Chernobyl. The risks decrease as time passes and as one gets farther from the source of the radiation. However, the health of the people near the scene of the accident will be in danger for many years.

At the time Unit 4 caught fire, there were few details about the accident. Henry Wagner, a professor of radiation health sciences at Johns Hopkins University in Baltimore, Maryland, described some of the medical effects of radiation. People exposed to extreme radiation may feel sick to their

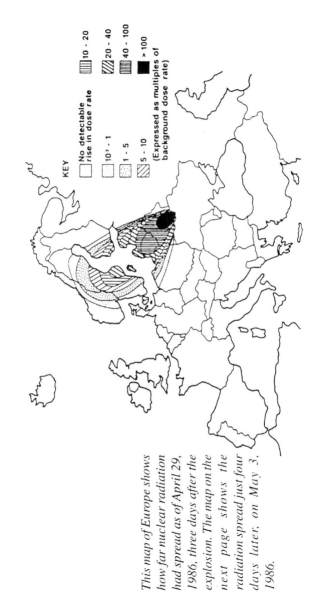

KEY

No detectable rise in dose rate

10³ - 1

1 - 5

5 - 10

10 - 20

20 - 40

40 - 100

> 100

(Expressed as multiples of background dose rate)

This map of Europe shows how far nuclear radiation had spread as of April 29, 1986, three days after the explosion. The map on the next page shows the radiation spread just four days later, on May 3, 1986.

37

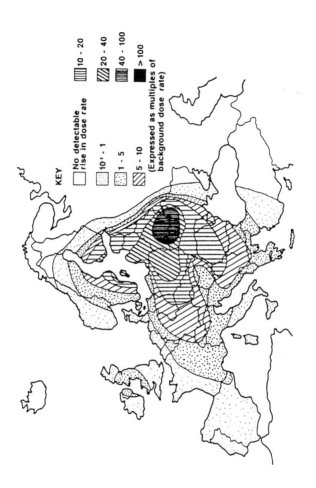

KEY

	No detectable rise in dose rate
	10^{-1} - 1
	1 - 5
	5 - 10
	10 - 20
	20 - 40
	40 - 100
	>100

(Expressed as multiples of background dose rate)

stomachs. Others may bleed inside their bodies. The possibility of death is very real for those people if the exposure is immediate and continues over time.

People who live within three to four miles of the source of radiation will probably have serious stomach problems. For them, too, the possibility of death is serious. According to Wagner, people living five to seven miles from a nuclear disaster may feel ill but are not likely to die.

Farther from the source of radiation, the immediate risks are not as great. Still, the long-term medical problems can be serious. Exposure to radiation from a nuclear disaster can result in a higher risk of leukemia and other forms of cancer for thirty or more years. Teenagers who were young children or infants living near Chernobyl when it burst into flames may worry about their health for the rest of their lives.

Radiation has specific effects on specific parts of the body. Sores are common on skin that has been exposed directly to radiation. Radiation exposure can increase the risk of cancer in the liver, kidneys, lungs, and breasts. Immediate exposure can also cause hair loss and damage to the eyes. Bleeding in the brain (hemorrhaging) may result in death. Radiation poisoning can destroy the walls of the intestines. Exposure also can cause damage to male and female reproductive organs.

Large doses of radiation can harm the bones' ability to produce white blood cells. This means the body is less able to fight infection. Because radiation exposure can affect a person's genes, birth defects may occur in the next generation. Many people exposed to radiation complain of stress.

In the spring of 1986, directly after the accident, the immediate and long-term medical consequences were unclear. Dr. Marvin Goldman, a professor of radiation biology at the University of California at Davis, indicated that stress may have been the most serious medical consequence of the disaster. Dr. Goldman was involved in a project to study the effects of radiation released at Chernobyl. He said, "I don't know of any radiation-caused illness in the area."

Not all experts agree that radiation from Chernobyl had so little effect on the people who lived nearby. Some studies show that the incidence of cancer has increased in contaminated areas. There is also evidence that indicates that children born to mothers who were pregnant at the time of the disaster—or who continued to live in contaminated areas during their pregnancies—are weaker than children in clean areas.

Other reports suggest that thousands of people living near Chernobyl have had health problems. Thousands of residents of Belarus (population: ten million) have suffered anemia, tuberculosis, cancer, and other disorders as a result of the nuclear accident.

"The medical and biological consequences of Chernobyl appear much more serious than had been expected during the first five years," said Dr. Tamara V. Belookaya of the Institute of Radiation Medicine in the Soviet Union.

She said that the medical fallout from Chernobyl has been very serious. People living in contaminated areas suffer from three times as much illness as people in unaffected areas.

Chapter 9

As it turned out, April 26, 1986 was not the only day that accidents would rattle the Chernobyl Nuclear Power Plant.

A water leak occurred on August 10, 1991. Two months later, a fire broke out over one of the two reactors that remained in operation. Because of those accidents and the 1986 partial meltdown, Ukraine's Parliament voted on October 29, 1991 to close the plant by 1993.

Then another fire broke out at the plant a few days later on November 1, 1991. Kiev and surrounding areas in Ukraine and Belarus were forced to explore and develop another primary source of energy.

The explosion at Chernobyl and then the closing of the plant came as a great blow to the Russian government. They had high hopes for Chernobyl. They had envisioned a truly modern plant, supplying energy to millions of people.

One Russian newspaper said there was evidence that the leaders had tried to make the disaster seem less serious than it really was. The newspaper had reported that thousands of people were put at risk because the government did not act immediately to protect those who lived and worked in contaminated areas.

Among other things, the Russian newspaper indicated that from 1986 through 1989, some 2 million tons of contaminated milk and 47,500 tons of contaminated meat were shipped out of the region to be sold elsewhere.

The article also reported that thousands of Chernobyl workers and their families were at risk when they were moved to the new town of Slavutich. According to the Russian newspaper, the town had been built in another area that the government knew was contaminated.

Only a few government officials were brave enough to speak the truth about the nuclear disaster at Chernobyl. The Ukrainian health minister Yuri Spizhenko estimated that six thousand to eight thousand people have died in the Ukraine alone as a result of fallout from Chernobyl.

It is unlikely that an accurate count of the deaths can ever be made.

Chapter 10

Like the rest of the world, the Soviet people learned some difficult lessons from the Chernobyl disaster. Sometimes nuclear power comes at a high cost.

The number of deaths and illnesses from the accident can never be counted accurately. But there is no question that the lives of thousands of people throughout the Soviet Union were affected when Unit 4 caught fire on April 26, 1986. That April dawn will be remembered.

Like other disasters and extraordinary events, Chernobyl turned many ordinary people into heroes. The efforts of Lieutenant Colonel Telyatnikov and his firefighters were truly heroic. They did the job they had to do, never questioning the grave danger they faced that April morning. Some people view Dr. Robert Gale as a great hero because of the bone marrow work he did in the weeks and months after the disaster.

There are many other heroes, including the helicopter pilots and the six hundred thousand workers who risked their lives to clean up after the disaster. And then there are the brave children who have been carefully watched and treated at clinics like the Diagnostic Center for Radiation Medicine or the Institute of Radiation Medicine. Some of them have leukemia. Others are disfigured by burns. Despite their visible and invisible scars, many are too young to remember the day Unit 4 blew at Chernobyl.

A young boy named Sergei could not quickly forget that April day. Two months after the disaster, the eleven-year-old Russian boy told a young American friend what it was like when Chernobyl caught fire.

Sergei had been at the plant, playing in a room for children, when the reactor caught fire. He was waiting to see his father, who worked at the power station. Sergei told his friend that when the walls collapsed, he was the only one who wasn't buried in the rubble. Sergei was badly burned; he had stopped to rescue an infant before running to safety outside.

Soviet officials have never reported that children were present at Chernobyl when the plant went up in flames. That possibility is one of the many stories of Chernobyl that may yet be told or remain a mystery forever.

Bibliography

Ladies' Home Journal, "The Children of Chernobyl," October 1986.

Life, "Witness to Disaster: An American Doctor at Chernobyl," August 1986.

Los Angeles Times, "Izvestia Details Pattern of Lies in Chernobyl Cover-Up," April 25, 1992.

National Geographic, "Chernobyl—One Year After," May 1987.

The New York Times, "Chernobyl Said to Affect Health of Thousands in Soviet Region," November 3, 1991.

The New York Times Magazine, "Chernobyl: Five Years Later the Danger Persists," April 14, 1991.

Newsweek, "A Fearful Flight from Chernobyl," May 19, 1986.

Newsweek, "Jitters on the Front Line," June 16, 1986.

Newsweek, "The Lessons of Chernobyl,"
April 27, 1987.

Newsweek, "In Chernobyl's Grim
Shadow," June 29, 1987.

Newsweek, "Chernobyl's Legacy," May
7, 1990.

People, "An Eyewitness to Disaster,"
May 19, 1986.

Science, "Reactor Explodes Amid Soviet
Silence," May 16, 1986.

Time, "Deadly Meltdown," August 14,
1989.